Discovering and Developing the Best of Me

A Self Help Book

Building Confidence, Self-Worth, Helping You Establish Your Dreams

Collette Neves

Discovering and Developing the Best of Me
Copyright © 2018 by Collette Neves

All rights reserved. No part of this book may be reproduced or transmitted in any form or by any means without written permission from the author.

ISBN - 9780578204758

Printed in USA by 48HrBooks (www.48HrBooks.com)

Dedication

I dedicate this book to anyone who has uncertainties regarding their self-worth or have forgotten their true value due to circumstances and obstacles of life. The Greater one resides in you; therefore, greatness is within you.

Keep Discovering Yourself

Collette Neves

Table of Contents

Foreword 5

Acknowledgements 7

Introduction 8

Chapter 1 9

Chapter 2 11

Chapter 3 13

Chapter 4 15

Chapter 5 17

Chapter 6 19

Chapter 7 21

Chapter 8 23

Chapter 9 24

Testimony 25

Conclusion 26

Profession 27

Foreword

I was first introduced to Collette Neves by her grandmother as a young girl and later re-introduced to her by her mother, as a young woman seeking for her purpose with God. When getting to know Collette as a Woman of God, we shared at one point in time the same career path on different levels. We often would speak on how our paths would cross but not knowing the true connection of meeting each other. As we continue to share our lives with our families, we both were walking in the direction of similar paths. The similar paths walked led us both to our true purpose in God; Collete path led her to speak and teach the principles of God's purpose for your life.

There is a profound saying *"Look within yourself to discover your true purpose for life,"* but Collette Neves understand your starting point is with Elohim "God" your creator and his purpose for your life.

"Before I formed you in the womb I knew[a] you before you were

born I set you apart;

I appointed you as a prophet to the nations." **Jeremiah 1:5**

Collette is a woman who personifies her worth in Jesus Christ through the Abounding of Grace in continually reaching the greater heights of success and influence. She loves people and loves encouraging them, challenging them, and cheering on their spiritual development in the Word of Jesus Christ. She understands as society thoughts and ways of teaching and developing a purpose for one is not fulfilling God's true purpose for one's life. The thought of society is saying that your validation of your purpose is through man, did not align with her understanding of who God is in her life.

There is another saying that states *"My validation is not in man,"* and many replies; because my Identity is in Christ Jesus." The saying of the words speaks to self-worth and who is the validator of your worth.

This book brings forth the true teachings of how to identify your true purpose through spiritual growth, which will bring forth the attributes of self-worth; validation of the true purpose of God

God Bless you as you speak, teach and pray, and may your life be empowered through the Holy Spirit, reflecting the fullness of God purpose through grace and mercy in your life.

Minister Debra D Langhorne

Acknowledgements

I acknowledge my Lord and Savior Jesus Christ for using me as a vessel to uplift and encourage others. I am grateful to God for being a Father to the fatherless, loving me unconditionally, and being sovereign as the head of life. Without You, I am nothing. Thank you for allowing me to be the apple of your eye and making me a master piece.

To my loving and supportive family, this book came to fruition because of you. Thanks to you for your prayers, patience, input, and for keeping me grounded; you are my solid rock.

To Apostle Mark Jones and Lady Lisa Jones, Thank You, for your continued support of impartation, guidance, and development.

To my sisters Thembi Bryant and Loretta Harvey, thank you for your prayers, encouragement, and love. I am grateful you are in my life.

Introduction

Do you find yourself feeling inadequate?

Do you need help overcoming not feeling worthy of yourself?

Do you find yourself in an unbalanced state?

Hopefully, as you read this book, you will discover and identify your true purpose in life. It will help to develop you to realize your potential to grow, evolve, and to increase effectiveness. It will advance you from a lower to a higher state, thus giving you a sense of self-worth through building your self-esteem and self-respect. Self-discipline is great for improvement which will tie into your self-mastery; the power to control your actions, impulses and/or emotions. Trust me, this is a daily process; however, it can be done with the holy spirit, your consistency and the renewing of your mind.

I decided to write this book because I believe as woman we wear many hats. And, because we are nurturers, we bear a lot and love to help family, friends, and even strangers (some would call this taking on many projects). However, we tend to forget about ourselves in this process; always putting ourselves on the back burner. Of course, I get it; if you were a single parent like myself or a wife, the family tends to come first. But, we must provide self-worth and self-care in this equation.

In the upcoming chapters, you will find affirmations to build your self-esteem, steps on self-discipline and suggestions on self-care.

Chapter One
Validation

Receiving and giving validation is of high importance. Growing up as a child, my parents were liberal in this area of my life., -However, you don't have to seek validation from others, you can build up yourself. When validation is not given by the parent or guardian, it can be used as an ulterior motive or manipulation by someone, causing an unbalanced state within your emotions, which can result in disruptive patterns into adulthood. Validation confirms value to the person; it communicates he is worthwhile, which helps form his identity.

For example, examine validation from a natural point of view. You have a plant or flower which we know both requires water and may need sunlight to blossom depending on the plant or flower. You would then proceed to give this plant water and the proper nutrients it needs to flourish and grow. This is validation illustrated, however, if validation (sun and water) is not given it becomes neglected, wither, and die. Or, when the weeds come (manipulation or ulterior motive), it will either entangle itself or stunt its growth; causing the plant or flower to become something else which usually dies. From a spiritual perspective, the word of God encourages us as dear friends to build ourselves up in our most holy faith and pray in the Holy Spirit. Jude 1:20 NIV.

You may be asking how to build yourself up in my most holy faith? One of the ways you can build yourself up in your most holy faith is by praying in the Holy Spirit. As a matter of fact, it is one of the most powerful ways. Praying in the Holy Spirit is praying to God in your heavenly language. So many times, we ignore ourselves, or put ourselves on auto pilot through the busyness of life. Try practicing self-care, which comes from a place of self-understanding and affirmation. God demonstrated to us affirmation through love when He sent His only son to die for our sins.

As previously stated, it is good to receive and give validation. Having help from others is a great part of the equation.

Below are some steps to make yourself a more central part of your own validation.

1. Be grateful and celebrate the good things about you, even your imperfections. Learn to embrace them as they are unique, and you are God's masterpiece He doesn't create junk.

2. Think positive about yourself; controlling your emotions to reflect your inner most being from a place of radiate light.

3. Remind yourself daily about your warm attributes. Examples:
   I am beautiful.
   I approve of myself, I love myself deeply and fully.
   I am valuable.
   I am the apple of God's eye.

Affirmation: I am a radiant beauty full of charm and grace.

Chapter Two
Positive Perception

Everyone has heard of the question, "Is the glass half full or half empty?" Both answers are correct, because they are not contradictory. The glass is half empty and half full at the same time. The focus of the question is not about the state of the glass, but about the perception of the observer. Positive perception is looking at things from a positive light; redirecting your thoughts, changing your mindset, and shifting your view to a more empowered one to overcome all situations and challenges. Your perception is based on how you see things, and what you believe. Your perspective and belief are based on your thoughts. When you change your perception, you eventually change your reality. This is the power of positive thinking and its importance to applying it daily. Positive thinking works better when you apply it before situations go wrong. Sometimes, this is not the case and you are at a point where your situation has already gone wrong and you need to apply positive thinking.

Imagine the company you work for is laying off employees, I know the first thought is 'what am I going to do.' First, do not give into any negative thoughts even though this may come as a shock. Lean on the source (God) and change your perception to reflect what is transpiring. Then, prepare your resume to highlight updated new roles or tasks you've accomplished for the next career. This situation lends the opportunity to discover your true passion, return to school to enhance your skill set, or become an entrepreneur. Whatever the case, trust in the source (God), and He will open the door and make your path plain. Through the process, the negative thoughts may arise, but the word of God says, *"cast your cares on the Lord and he will sustain you"* (Psalm 55:22) NIV.

Possessing a positive perception is something you must practice daily. It requires discipline and a positive attitude; the more you apply them, the easier it becomes. You must remain optimistic even when circumstances do not work out or is delayed. Speak what you want to see, call those things that are not as though they were, meaning having the God kind of faith as Mark 11:24 *encourages "What things soever ye desire, when ye pray, believe that ye receive them, and ye shall have them."* Once you believe, you have to speak this. Follow the method that God used; he spoke, and it came to pass! We speak his word, and it comes to pass.

Below is a list of steps to guide you with the practice of positive perception.

1. Renew your mind daily with truths of scripture

2. Change the way you see things, constantly shift your thoughts to positive – getting rid of negative thoughts. Have a grateful heart; a grateful heart protects you from negative thinking.

3. Push your mind forward to think about the solution of what you want to achieve next in the situation. Learn from your past mistakes and concentrate on how you can overcome to be successful the next time. Remember, delay is not denial.

Affirmation: My ability to conquer my challenges is limitless, my potential to succeed is infinite.

Chapter Three
Emotional Control

Emotions manifest in both a positive and negative sense and are definitely controllable. There is a saying which communicates how people are driven daily by their emotions. With this, I suggest controlling your emotions and not allowing your emotions to control you, especially the negative ones. Emotional control refers primarily to attempts by an individual to manage the experience, or expressions and responses of emotions. For example, anger or fear will set your heart racing and feelings of joy or happiness will put a smile on your face. It's very important to control your negative emotions. If you find yourself becoming angry in a situation, or if there are triggers that may set you off from something that someone says or does, or maybe an incident that is out of your control, there could be a root issue that you have not addressed (maybe from childhood, broken relationship, abandonment, or something from your past that you have not been delivered from).

When we act on negative emotions too quickly, we often end up making unwise decisions. Negative emotions like rage, envy, or bitterness tend to spiral out of control, and these emotions are best met with a sense of moderation and a logical perspective. Emotions are powerful and real to the individual experiencing them. Emotions are also a helpful indicator of what is transpiring in our hearts. Scripture reads, *"above all else, guard your heart, for everything you do flows from it"* Proverbs 4:23 (NIV). God creates us as emotional beings; He creates us in His image. With that being said, it behooves us to be vigilant in managing emotions rather than allowing the emotions to manage us. God is looking at how we respond. Yes, I know this may involve much practice, but your end result will be more rewarding. For example, when we feel angry, it is important to be able to stop, identify that we are angry, examine our hearts to determine why we are angry, and then proceed in a way God would want us to respond in, LOVE. Scripture declares we are to be controlled by the Holy Spirit, not by our emotions. James 1:19 states, *"my dear brothers and sisters take note of this: Everyone should be quick to listen, slow to speak, and slow to become angry"* (NIV).

Below are a few steps to help guide you on controlling your emotions.

1. Be slow to react– take a deep breath and stabilize the overwhelming impulse, continue to breathe deeply for five minutes, while feeling your muscles relax and your heart rate returns to normal.

2. Ask for divine guidance – faith is the saving grace in our darkest moments.

3. See the bigger picture – every happening in our lives, whether good or bad, serves a higher purpose.

Affirmation: Everything that is happening now is happening for my ultimate good.

Chapter Four
The Discovery

This chapter is strategically about finding your true purpose in life, your passion. Passion is defined as a strong amorous feeling or desire. Passion is seen as something we take pleasure in doing, which normally come with ease and flows like water. When we operate in our passion it is fulfilling and the task is enjoyable. Your passion can be anything that simultaneously challenges you, intrigues you, and motivates you. Contrary to the idea that doing what you love makes work effortless, a passion puts you to work. It is what you are willing to sacrifice your leisure and pleasures for.

Examining purpose more closely, you will see that purpose is the reason for which something exists or is done. Specifically, purpose can guide life decisions, influence behavior, shape your goals, offer a sense of direction, and create meaning. I believe everyone has purpose in life, whether it's connected to your family, your career, your ministry, or your community. Meeting the needs of others and contributing to a higher purpose provide a healthier outlook on life. Discovering your passion and purpose will clearly be revealed to you when you dwell in the audience of one with God. Be true to yourself and find out what drives you. Is there anything that touches you deeply that it propels you? Or something you find yourself always being concerned about? A powerful purpose can come from a powerful pain. Find out what energizes you, what you are willing to sacrifice, and who you are driven to help. In truth, ask God to guide you through the process. He will make provision for your needs. When He gives vision, He will give provision.

The bible states: *"I will instruct you and teach you in the way you should go; I will counsel you with my loving eye on you". Psalm 32:8 NIV*

Below are steps to finding your purpose and passion.

1. Commune with God and ask Him to reveal your purpose in life.

2. Ask yourself questions which lead to growth. Ask yourself what am I thinking? What else is possible? What do I love to do and why?

3. Identify patterns and themes in your life that you enjoy. What have they prepared you to do? What do others come to you for advice about? Consider, what comes easy to you as breathing but is a struggle for others?

Affirmation: Follow your passion; it will lead you to your purpose.

Chapter Five
Set the Goal

Let us recap for a moment: now that you are validating and building up yourself, looking at circumstances from a positive perception, controlling your emotions, and discovering your passion to fulfill your purpose in life, it is time to proceed with setting your goals. Setting a goal can be personal or professional. Goal setting is a powerful process for motivating yourself to turn your vision into reality.

Athletes, successful business people, and achievers in all fields set goals. Setting goals give you long term vision and short-term motivation. By knowing precisely what you want to achieve, you know where you must concentrate your efforts. Another benefit for goal setting focuses your acquisition of knowledge and helps you to organize your time and resources. Set precise, clearly defined goals that you can measure and take pride in the achievement of those goals. Then, you will see progress in what might previously have seemed a long pointless grind. Your self-confidence will elevate, as well as the recognition of your ability and competence in achieving the goals you have set.

With this in mind, explore how to set smart goals. I learned by reading the Shape book by Erik Rees to set S.M.A.R.T goals, which means be specific, measurable, attainable, relevant and time bound. Once you know what you want to achieve, commit. Set goals that motivate you and write them down; this causes them to feel tangible. Put your completion time next to each goal, whether it's two weeks, two months, or two years. Then, plan the steps you must take to realize your goal and mark each one off as you work through them.

Do not succumb to fear or disappointment if you must adjust your goals time frame, for this reveals determination. Do not be afraid of the unknown; remember you sat in the counsel of God to reveal your passion and purpose for your life. Stand firm on His word, trust and believe. God will prepare you, preserve you, position you, and protect you. The word of God states, *"for the vision is yet for an appointed time, but at the end it shall speak, and not lie: though it tarry, wait for it; because it will surely come, it will not tarry"* (Habakkuk 2:3) KJV.

Below are some steps to guide you through your process of Goal Setting.
1. Set daily goals to ensure you reach your long-term goals.

2. Keep your mind energized, clear, and focused on the process of your goals. Focus is never lost, just redirected.

3. Clearly visualize the attainment of your goals.

Affirmation: Live in the present, never dwelling on the past and take action to ensure a wonderful future.

Chapter Six
Accountability

Accountability is the quality or state of being accountable; especially an obligation or willingness to accept responsibility or to account for one's actions. Accountability is a personal choice to rise above one's circumstance and demonstrate the ownership necessary for achieving desired results. Alignment with your goals is crucial and having an accountability partner makes achieving these goals a reality. This would be someone to help you keep the commitments you have identified regarding your goals. Being consistent, trustworthy, and transparent is healthy and rewarding in this type of relationship. Don't view your accountability partner as controlling, manipulative or someone simply giving orders. Once again, they are to keep you aligned with truth, guide you through the process, and if they are led by the Holy Spirit, they will lead you to Christ in your result.

The accountability partner should support your efforts. This will help you remain focus and positive on the best most important parts of your life. Be sure you are clear about what you ideally want help with. What is your purpose? And what do you want to get out of the relationship? For example, feedback, reporting progress or opinions about goals, problem solving on items and issues when they arise, or someone to brainstorm ideas.

You also want to make sure the accountability partner fits your desired qualities. For instance, respect for other's values, open-minded, objective, nonjudgmental of your goals, and willing to communicate with compassionate honesty. Once you decide on the right accountability partner, work out the structure and logistic, such as the frequency of meeting. How will you meet; in person, via phone, or video conference? How long will the meeting last? Also, consider the flow of the meeting.

Accountability partners can consist of one person or more than one person for different areas of your life you would like to be held accountable like health, exercise, personal, professional or financial.

There are coaches, mentors, pastors, family members and even on-line groups that can help you accomplish your goals.

The word of God states: *"Sanctify them through thy truth: thy word is truth". John 17:17 KJV*

Below are steps to guide you through your journey of accountability.

1. Have the right mindset – remain open, teachable, and transparent.

2. Have an accountability partner with integrity, maintain confidentiality, and is edifying.

3. Educate yourself on your goals; make the conscious effort to hold yourself accountable to your goals.

Affirmation: Success is not achieved alone; you should have an accountability partner. Surround yourself with people that encourage you to do better.

Chapter Seven
Consistent Pattern

We are now on our way to the finish line. Commitment to a daily set of actions, aligned with specific goals, and consistency is the key. When you take consistent actions, you will eventually build small successes along the way. Consistency is about developing the persistence and patience necessary to stick with your goal until it manifests. As you set your goals, lay them before the Lord. The word of God reads, *"And let us not be weary in well doing: for in due season we shall reap, if we faint not."* Galatians 6:9 KJV. This verse is not just limited to your goals; this can be your thoughts, desires, hopes, and dreams. As I have prayed this verse over my family, it encourages me to push through when unexpected situations arise. I come back to this truth and it stills my soul. We should bring our goals before the Lord and seek His will and direction that He may lead and guide us accordingly.

Write down your goals. Written promises to yourself can strengthen the internal fortitude needed to complete a challenging task. Post reminders and a checklist in a visible location (like a daily planner, wall calendar, or a note on your desktop computer), these can be an effective motivator for follow through. Trust and walk out your goals. A goal is a statement of faith. Setting goals help you stay connected and it helps with continued growth.

Below are steps to help you trust and walk out your journey while being consistent.

1. Put God first, you can't go wrong when your desires are His.

2. Again, jot down your goals making them tangible; give them an end date. Having no date puts them in a category of a wish list.

3. Include positive affirmations or belief statements in your goal setting.

Affirmation: Positivity drives us when we feel we can no longer continue. Get it right with goal setting and consistency.

Chapter Eight
Never Give in or Give Up

As you go through the journey of building your self-worth, exercising self-discipline, and controlling your emotions, never abandon your process. It does not matter what circumstance arise, or what people may say. Allow only God to define you and not people or your circumstance. When obstacles come, remember the discussion regarding the controlling of your emotions. God is looking at how we respond in LOVE and this helps with our growth and character.

Remaining teachable helps us grow, evolve, and improve. With this mindset, you will expand to reach your potential as the masterpiece God created you to be. Your growth is your personal responsibility. Jesus is the root out of your dry ground. Remember whatever you accompany you become so no negative thoughts. Durability is a result of growth. You may bend in circumstances but realize you are still standing. Be flexible; you will grow regardless of what transpires around you. There is more to you than what is visible, therefore operate in your fullest potential. The word of God says: *"Be ye strong therefore and let not your hands be weak: for your work shall be rewarded."* 2 Chronicles 15:7 KJV.

Below are some steps so you will Never Give in or Give Up.

1. Stay humble and keep your faith, realizing you always have room to grow.

2. Continue to learn something new every time you engage in using your gifts and talents, your work, and your relationship.

3. Have a heart open to instructions as well as constructive criticism (push through).

Affirmation: Never Give Up. Set a goal and go for it.

Chapter Nine
You are Valuable

I hope by now you know that you are valuable. You were made in the image of God. Through Christ, you are the apple of His eye. You are God's masterpiece.

I am here to encourage and edify you. There is greatness inside of you, you have so much potential and your attributes are astonishing.

I appreciate you, thank you for your joyous spirit, your smile, and support. Our time together has been of the essence and I am truly grateful for our friendship.

Wow, this has been an exciting journey. Remember to implement self-care in your life as well. Self-care fuels you up. When you are filled, you can fuel others. If you are depleted, you will be unable to give of yourself. So, whatever you enjoy doing that rejuvenates, you go for it. Soaking in a hot tub, going to the spa, getting a massage, reading, walking on the beach, exercise, or just relaxing, be good to yourself.

Testimony

Unwelcomed pain can sometimes send you through turbulence that's unexplainable. However, it's one of life lessons that taught me self-worth, self- discipline, and self- mastery. During a cultivating period in my life, I learned to be in a place of contentment through submission to the Father and staying in His
presence. It was through intimacy that the Holy Spirit revealed the areas of my life where I was broken and damaged.

Pure worship and walking by faith into uncomfortable territories, that I never let God into, is where I began to face myself head on. I had to abandon who I thought I was and the history of what I lived, to become the true divine person
God designed. It wasn't easy for me to abandon my survival tactics, nevertheless, in-order for me to fulfill purpose and come into alignment with God, it was necessary.

When you come to the realization of who you are and why God has need of you, it
changes your perspective. Allowing the Father to teach me how to deal with unwelcomed pain has taught me to love more, to see people how He sees them, to forgive immediately, and to pray without ceasing.

Mastering these areas of my life has brought calmness to my soul. I choose to be unique by replacing pain with love, it's the gift that God commanded we use.

Signed,

My pain made me Beautiful.

Conclusion

The reason I wrote this book was for each one of you to discover and develop the best of you. Remember you are not what happens to you, you are not what someone says about you, only God can define you. On your journey don't allow time to harass you, it is all in God's timing and His complete plan. Be careful not to discredit or short change yourself; don't be imprisoned by your imperfections. Be steadfast, unmovable, always abounding in the things of Christ.

Love,

Collette Neves

PROFESSIONS

The below are professions that may be used to strengthen you and build your faith.
I am what God says I am.
I have what God says I have.
I can do what God says I can do.
Greater is he that's in me than he that is in the world. (1 John 4:4)
I've been delivered from the kingdom of darkness. (Col. 1:13)
I'm seated far above all principality and power. (Eph. 1:21)
The devil is under my feet. (Eph. 1:22)
I'm a kingdom and a priest to serve God. (Rev. 5:10)
The Lord delights in my well-being. (Ps. 35:27)
All my needs are supplied. (Phil. 4:19)
I must give, and it will be given to me (Lu. 6:38)
The windows of heaven are open to me. (Mal. 3:10)
I have life in abundance. (John 10:10)
I leave an inheritance to my kids, kids. (Pr. 13:22)
My seed is blessed. (Deut. 28:4)
I'm a lender not a borrower. (Deut. 28:12)
I'm blessed in the city and field. (Deut. 28:3)
I'm the head and not the tail. (Deut. 28:13)
I have favor with God and all men. (Luke 2:52)
Whatsoever I do prosper. (Ps. 1:3)
I flourish like a tree beside water. (Ps. 1:3)
I'm healed by the stripes of Jesus. (1 Peter 2:24)
Jesus took my infirmities and bare my sickness (Matt. 8:17)
I'm the righteousness of God in Christ Jesus. (II Cor. 5:21)
The Lord's mercy is new everyday towards me. (Lam. 3:23)
I have peace. (Phil. 4:7)
I don't have a spirit of fear, but of love, power and a sound mind.
 (II Tim. 1:7)
Because God is my dwelling, no evil shall befall me, nor any plague come nigh my dwelling. (Ps. 91:9-10)
Angels are protecting me. (Ps. 91:11)
I can do all things through Christ. (Phil. 4:13)
No weapon formed against me shall prosper. (Is. 54:17)
God is for me, so it doesn't matter who's against me. (Rom. 8:31)
I'm seated in heavenly places in Christ. (Eph. 2:6)

ABOUT THE AUTHOR

Collette Neves is a certified Life Coach with credentials from Manifest Theological Institute in Tampa, Florida. Collette is the CEO and Founder of U Blossom LLC. She is passionate about encouraging, enhancing, and uplifting partners through personal challenges. While working twenty-three years in the finance industry, she served ten of those years in leadership roles providing development, support, and motivational coaching to employees. During that time, her passion was ignited to meet the needs of others by giving transformational life experiences. She believes there is greatness in us all, for those who has the Greater one residing within. Collette commits to helping partners rid their fears, change negative mind-sets, and set powerful specific goals to achieve. Together we will cheer on your success!

Made in United States
Orlando, FL
30 May 2023